W9-BVP-986

EGYPT
10NP
FUJEIRA
by Sherra G. Edgar

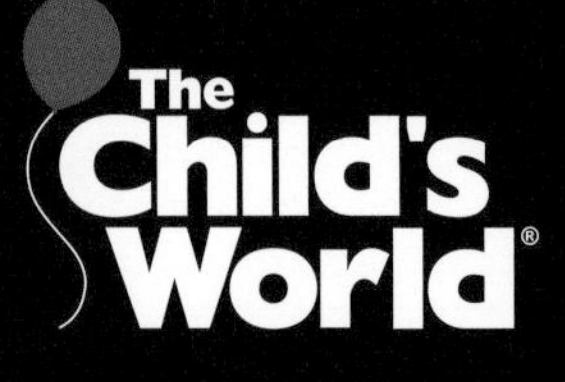

Published by The Child's World®
1980 Lookout Drive • Mankato, MN 56003-1705
800-599-READ • www.childsworld.com

Acknowledgments
The Child's World®: Mary Berendes, Publishing Director
Red Line Editorial: Editorial direction
The Design Lab: Design
Amnet: Production

Design elements: Vladimir Wrangel/Shutterstock Images; Markau Mark/Shutterstock Images; Shutterstock Images

Photographs ©: iStockphoto, cover (right), 5, 13, 15, 20, 21, 25, 27, 28; Vladimir Wrangel/Shutterstock Images, cover (left center), 1 (bottom left), 18 (bottom left); Markau Mark/Shutterstock Images, cover (left bottom), 1 (bottom right); Shutterstock Images, cover (left top), 1 (top), 6–7, 8, 16, 17, 18 (top), 18 (bottom right), 26; Paul Prescott/Shutterstock Images, 10; Elzbieta Sekowska/Shutterstock Images, 11; Oleksandr Kalinichenko/Shutterstock Images, 12; Mido Semsem/Shutterstock Images, 22; Serg Dibrova/Shutterstock Images, 24; Patryk Kosmider/Shutterstock Images, 30

ISBN 9781634070423
LCCN 2014959735

Printed in the United States of America
PA02354

ABOUT THE AUTHOR

Sherra G. Edgar lives in Lumberton, Texas. She has taught primary school for 19 years and has written books for children for three years. Edgar enjoys spending time with family and friends, reading, and watching movies.

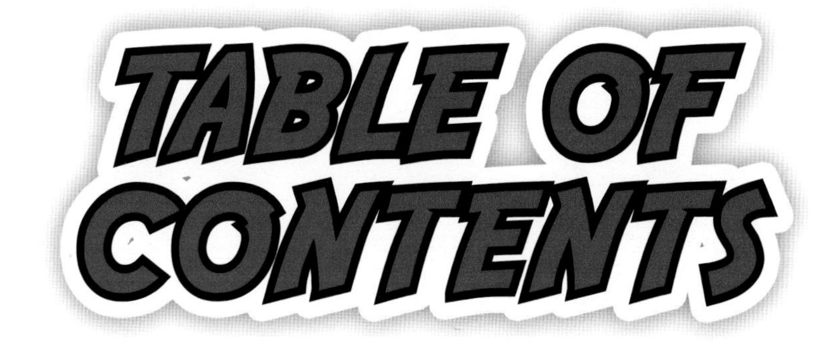
TABLE OF CONTENTS

ARCTIC OCEAN
ATLANTIC OCEAN
PACIFIC OCEAN
PACIFIC OCEAN
INDIAN OCEAN
SOUTHERN OCEAN
EGYPT
SCALE
0 1000 Miles
0 1000 KM
N
W
E
S
EGYPT
FUN FACT
ONE WORLD MANY COUNTRIES
10 NP
FUJEIRA
The Nile River flows across Egypt for 750 miles (1,207 km). Ninety-nine percent of Egyptians live along its banks. The land there is green and lush compared with the nearby desert.

CHAPTER 1

WELCOME TO EGYPT!

A warm spring breeze blows through the air. It is March 21. Egyptian families fill the parks. They are celebrating Sham el-Nessim. It is an ancient Egyptian holiday. The words *sham el-nessim* mean "sniffing the breeze."

Sham el-Nessim marks the beginning of spring. On this day, Egyptians enjoy picnic lunches at their favorite outdoor spots. Some even have picnics aboard boats on the Nile River.

Egypt is a modern nation, but children also learn about ancient traditions such as Sham el-Nessim. This holiday has been celebrated for thousands of years.

Egyptians load their picnic baskets with traditional food for this holiday. The baskets hold dried or pickled fish. They also contain *medames*. This food is an Egyptian bean.

In the cities, street vendors sell Egyptian foods. People listen to concerts throughout the day. Families watch traditional performances, such as the Horse Dance. In this dance, a horse prances, swishes its tail, and kicks its back legs to traditional music.

Sham el-Nessim is a day that Egyptian children look forward to every year. They live in a country with

a long history. It is home to one of the world's oldest civilizations. Many scientists believe Egypt's civilization dates back to around 3000 BC. Today it is a modern nation that is growing quickly.

Egyptians still travel across the desert using camels, as their ancestors did.

CHAPTER 2

THE LAND

The Red Sea is one of the world's warmest bodies of water. In the summer, the water can reach 85 degrees Fahrenheit (29°C).

Egypt is in northern Africa. Israel, Libya, and Sudan border Egypt. The Mediterranean Sea borders Egypt on the north. To the country's east is the Red Sea. The Suez Canal connects the two seas.

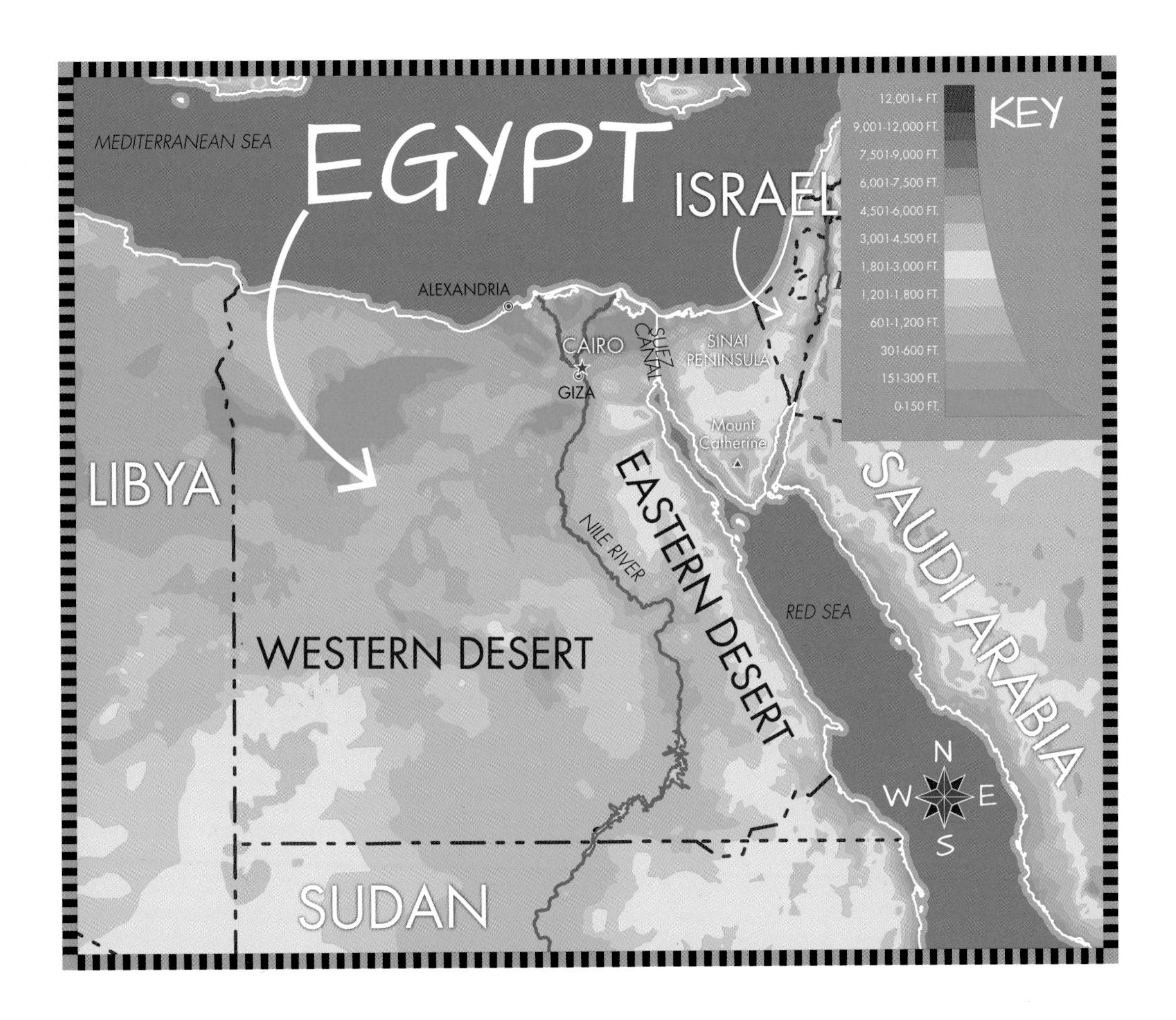

The Sinai **Peninsula** is in eastern Egypt. It is a piece of land shaped like a triangle. This peninsula connects Africa and Asia. Mountains tower over the southern part of the peninsula. It has Egypt's highest peak, Mount Catherine. In the north, the peninsula's land slopes down to the Mediterranean Sea.

The Nile River is important to Egypt. The river enters Egypt along its border with Sudan. From there, the Nile flows north and empties into the Mediterranean Sea. It provides most of Egypt's water.

Every summer the Nile River floods, and water covers the valleys. The floods provide water to growing plants. Without the floods, the soil would be too dry for plants to grow.

Egypt's land is mostly desert. It is hot during the day and cold at night. Only about 1 inch (2.5 cm) of rain falls each year. The Eastern Desert is between the Nile River and the

A truck drills for oil in the Sinai Peninsula.

The Nile River is the longest river in the world. It is about 4,132 miles (6,650 km) long and flows through ten African countries.

Red Sea. It has tall mountains and wadis, which are dry riverbeds. The Western Desert covers the land from Libya to the Nile. The land there is dry with rocks and sand.

Egypt has many natural resources. One of the most important is oil. Egypt is Africa's largest oil-producing country. It **exports** around 85,000 barrels each day. Egypt's oil comes from the Gulf of Suez, Sinai Peninsula, and deserts.

Another resource in Egypt is natural gas. Egypt is Africa's third-largest producer of natural gas. Most of the country's natural gas is found in the Western Desert and along the Nile. Egypt trades natural gas with countries in the Middle East and Europe.

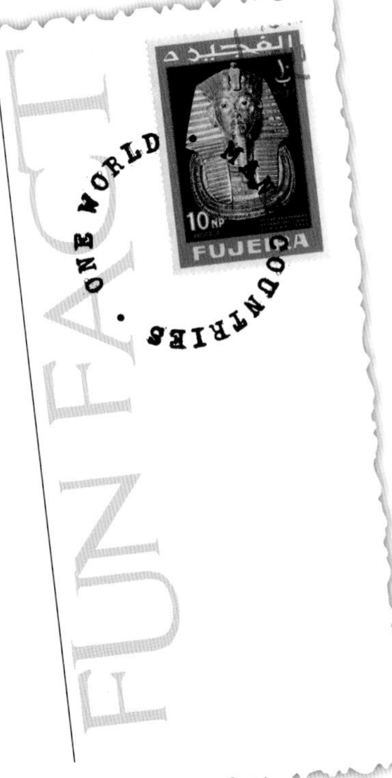

CHAPTER 3

In ancient Egypt there was only one ruler. He was called the pharaoh. The pharaoh made all decisions for the Egyptian people. Many pharaohs believed they were gods. They forced people to treat them like gods, too.

One of Egypt's most famous pharaohs was King Tutankhamen. He is often called King Tut. In this drawing, he is shown hunting birds.

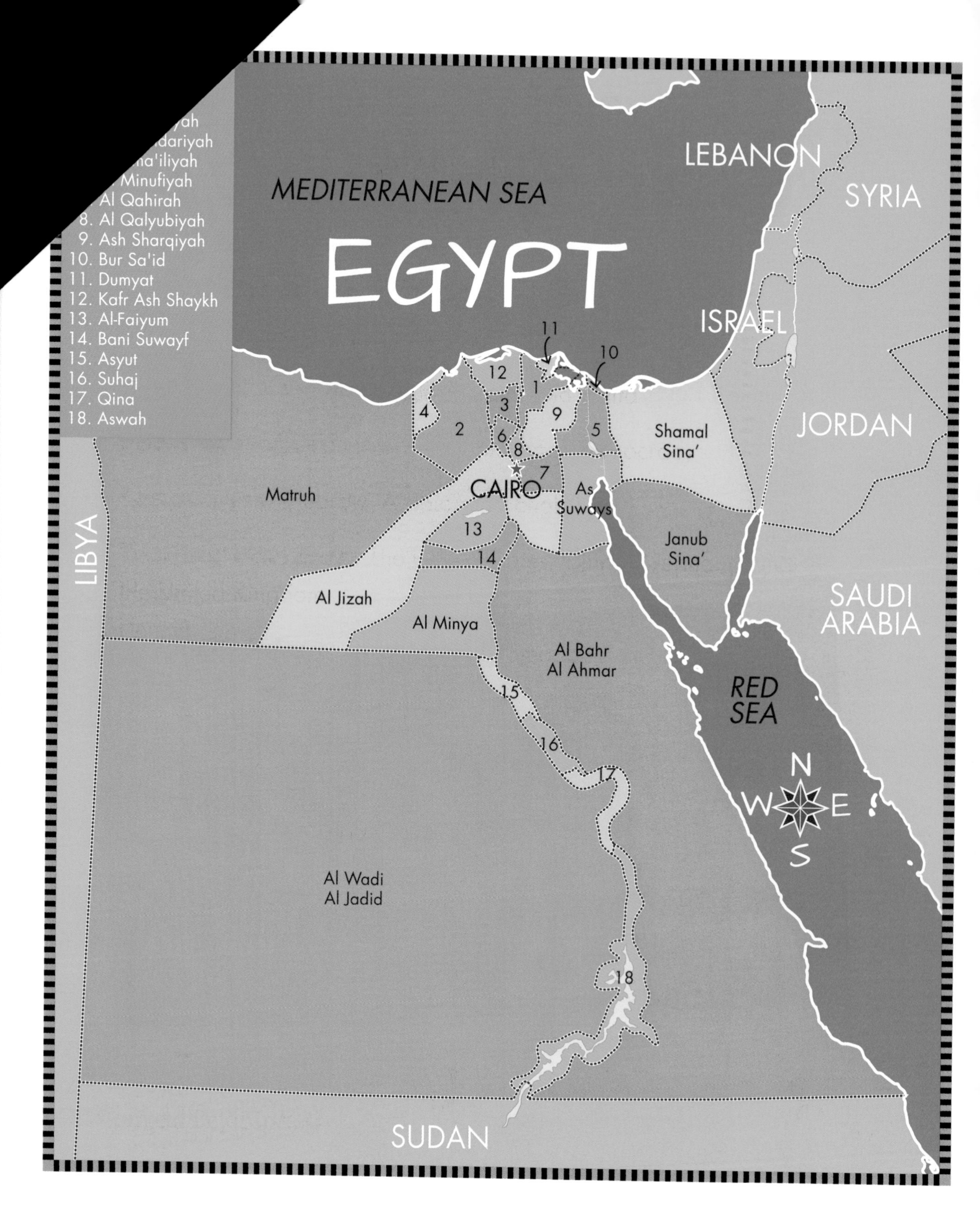
Minufiyah
Al Qahirah
8. Al Qalyubiyah
9. Ash Sharqiyah
10. Bur Sa'id
11. Dumyat
12. Kafr Ash Shaykh
13. Al-Faiyum
14. Bani Suwayf
15. Asyut
16. Suhaj
17. Qina
18. Aswah
MEDITERRANEAN SEA
EGYPT
LEBANON
SYRIA
ISRAEL
JORDAN
SAUDI ARABIA
LIBYA
SUDAN
RED SEA
Matruh
CAIRO
As Suways
Shamal Sina'
Janub Sina'
Al Jizah
Al Minya
Al Bahr Al Ahmar
Al Wadi Al Jadid
N
W
E
S

Today, Egypt's government is different. Egyptians elect their lawmakers and president. The president leads the country and also chooses the prime minister. The prime minister runs the government.

The president also chooses governors. They are in charge of the Egypt's governorates. A governorate is similar to a state. Egypt has 27 governorates. In almost every governorate live more than 1,000 people.

Many Egyptians are very involved with their government. This woman and thousands like her attend a political rally in 2011.

The Nile River runs through Cairo.

The Cairo Governorate is home to the nation's capital, Cairo. Cairo is Egypt's largest city. About 12 million people live there. It is the second-largest city in Africa. It has stood on the banks of the Nile River for more than 1,000 years.

Cairo is a mix of old and new. It has modern skyscrapers, shops, and restaurants. Older sections of the city have narrow streets and traditional markets. It also has about 400 historic palaces, museums, and **mosques**.

To the northwest of Cairo is the city of Alexandria. It is Egypt's second-largest city. About 4 million people live there. It has a busy port on the Mediterranean Sea.

The three Pyramids of Giza were built between 2575 BC and 2465 BC. Each pyramid was built for a different pharaoh. Their names were Khufu, Khafre, and Menkaure.

Giza is the third-largest city in Egypt. Ancient Egyptians built famous pyramids there. They served as tombs for important people, such as pharaohs.

Egypt's main industry is tourism. Thousands of tourists visit Egypt every year. Egypt is also known for its **textiles. They are made** with cotton grown in Egyptian fields. Farmers also grow rice, corn, wheat, and fruit. These are important exports. Egypt also trades its oil and natural gas with other countries.

FUN FACT
Giza is home to the Great Sphinx. It is a limestone statue with the face of a human and the body of a lion.
ONE WORLD • MANY COUNTRIES •
10NP
FUJEIRA
Egypt's currency
Egypt's flag

GLOBAL CONNECTIONS

People across the world use Egyptian inventions every day. Many of these inventions have been used for thousands of years. They have become so common that most people cannot imagine living without them.

One of these inventions is the calendar. The ancient Egyptians were the first people to create a calendar with 365 days. It had 12 months, and each month had 30 days. This calendar was the model for the modern calendar used today.

The Egyptians also invented the world's first door locks. Egyptians began using locks around 2000 BC. The wooden lock was bolted onto a door. To open it, a person would slide a long wooden key into the lock. The key released pins inside the lock, unlocking the door.

Makeup is another Egyptian invention. The Egyptians created eyeliner, eye shadow, body paint, and powders. The makeup had two jobs. It was meant to make a person look beautiful. Some kinds also protected the wearer from Egypt's harsh sun and wind. It is similar to what sunscreen does today.

CHAPTER 4

Egypt has been home to people for thousands of years. The main language Egyptians speak is Arabic. This is an ancient language. It has been spoken for thousands of years. Many Egyptians also speak English.

Egyptian children get ready to play a game of soccer in their neighborhood in Cairo.

Islam is the most common religion in Egypt. People who follow Islam are called Muslims. About 90 percent of Egyptians are Muslims. They worship their god Allah. Their holy book is the Koran. It has the writings of Muhammad. He is the founder of Islam.

Many of Egypt's holidays are Islamic holidays. Muharram is the Islamic New Year. It is a quiet holiday. People celebrate by reading from the Koran and reciting prayers. Mawlid an-Nabi is a holiday that celebrates Muhammad's birthday and the beginning of Islam.

Ramadan is the ninth month in the Islamic calendar. It is a month of **fasting** for Muslims. At the end of Ramadan, there is a holiday called Eid al-Fitr. Eid al-Fitr means "Festival of Breaking the Fast." Muslims celebrate by dressing up and decorating their homes. The children receive treats. Friends and families enjoy time together.

Eid al-Adha, or the "Feast of the Sacrifice," is an other important Islamic celebration. During Eid al-Adha, Muslims are encouraged to travel to Mecca. It is the holiest city of Islam and is in Saudi Arabia. For most Muslims, a trip to Mecca happens only once in their lifetime and is very special.

Egyptian children often receive lanterns as gifts during Ramadan. Streets are also decorated with lanterns during this holy month.

CHAPTER 5

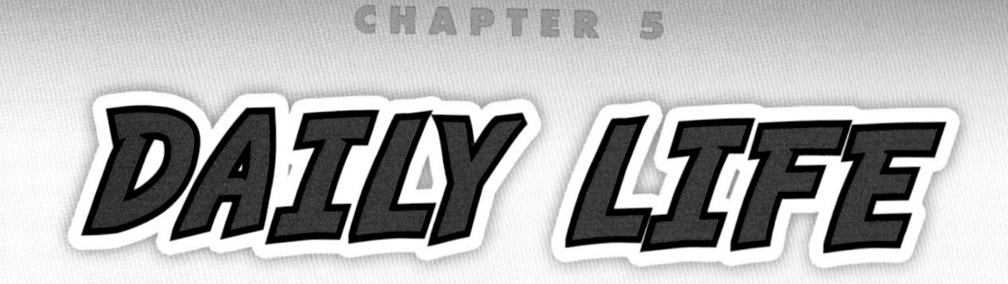

DAILY LIFE

Mosques have tall towers called minarets. A person called a *muezzin* goes to the top of a minaret to call Muslims to prayer.

Islam influences daily life in Egypt. In Islam, Friday is a day of rest. Schools, stores, and businesses are closed on Fridays. It is also common to hear a call to prayer five times a day. The call echoes throughout the cities.

Two boys wear traditional *djellabas* as they ride on a donkey cart in the Sahara Desert.

Islam also encourages people to wear **modest** clothing. Women often wear long, loose, black robes when leaving home. They usually wear *hijabs*, too. These veils cover the head, neck, and chest. Men wear *djellabas*. They are long, loose shirts. In cities, some people choose to wear clothing similar to that worn in the United States.

Food in Egypt has many different flavors. For breakfast, most people have tea, fruit, and bread with honey. Lunch is the main meal of the day. It is usually eaten late in the afternoon, around two or three o'clock. Egypt's national dish

People of Aswan, Egypt, shop in a traditional market in the town center.

is *koshari*. It has lentils, pasta, and rice topped with a spicy tomato sauce.

In the cities, Egyptians often live in apartments. They are modern and have indoor plumbing and electricity. In the country, many people live on farms. Their homes are made of mud bricks.

Modern apartments in Cairo

Farmers in the country can often walk from place to place. In the cities, people take cars, buses, and taxis. They can also ride the public rail system.

To relax, many Egyptians enjoy visiting coffee shops, called *ahwa*. There is often live music at *ahwas*. People get together to visit and drink coffee. Many visit outdoor markets or meet friends at restaurants and parks.

Sports are also a popular pastime. People living near the Nile River can go waterskiing, boating, and fishing. Football and beach handball are also popular sports to play and watch.

Fellahin are peasant farmers in Egypt. They form about half of the population along the Nile. Large groups of farmers walk to and from their fields every morning and afternoon.

Families are important to Egyptians. Just like families in other countries, Egyptian families like to spend time together. Children are considered a great blessing in Egypt. Parents work hard to give their children wonderful lives. They are the future of this ancient nation.

DAILY LIFE FOR CHILDREN

Egyptians value school. Children go to school for 12 years. Basic education in Egypt is preschool, elementary school, and secondary school.

At the end of secondary school, students receive a certificate. Next, students can choose what they would like to do. Some people attend college. They study to be doctors, business owners, teachers, and lawyers. Some students choose to learn a trade. They may study computers, electricity, or construction.

FAST FACTS

Population: 87 million

Area: 386,662 square miles (1,001,450 sq km)

Capital: Cairo

Largest Cities: Cairo, Alexandria, and Giza

Form of Government: Republic

Language: Arabic

Major Trading Partners: Italy, India, China, and the United States

Major Holidays: Muharram, Eid al-Fitr, and Eid al-Adha

National Dish: *koshari* (lentils, pasta, and rice topped with a spicy tomato sauce)

This girl lives in the desert near Hurghada, Egypt. She is a Bedouin, which is a group of people who move from place to place in the desert.

exports (EX-ports) Exports are food, clothing, or other goods that one country sells to other countries. Oil is one of Egypt's exports.

fasting (FAST-ing) Fasting is the act of not eating for religious reasons. Muslims fast during the month of Ramadan.

modest (MOD-ist) In clothing, modest means to not reveal a person's figure. Muslims often value modest clothing.

mosques (MOSKS) Mosques are Muslim places of worship. Muslims go to mosques to pray.

peninsula (puh-NIN-suh-lah) A peninsula is land that is surrounded by water on three sides. Egypt's land includes the Sinai Peninsula.

textiles (TEK-stiles) Textiles are woven or knit fabrics or cloths. Egyptians make many cotton textiles.

To Learn More

BOOKS

Arlon, Penelope. *Ancient Egypt*. New York: Scholastic, Inc., 2014.

Green, Roger Lancelyn. *Tales of Ancient Egypt*. New York: Puffin, 2013.

Putnam, James. *Pyramid*. New York: DK Pub., 2011.

WEB SITES

Visit our Web site for links about Egypt: **childsworld.com/links**

Note to Parents, Teachers, and Librarians: We routinely verify our Web links to make sure they are safe and active sites. So encourage your readers to check them out!

Index

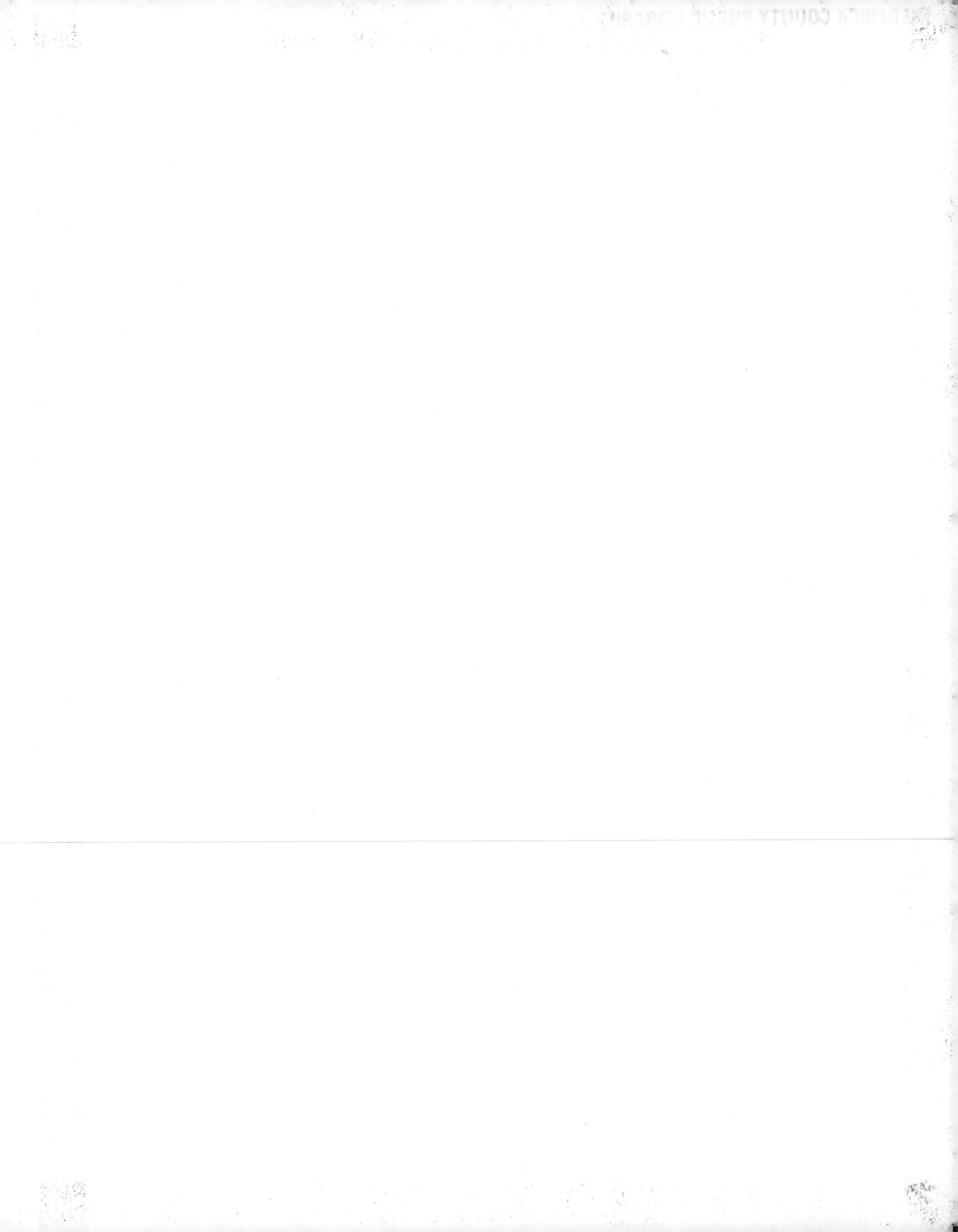